OF EARTHEN

MW00617797

SMOKE

By Sara Sutton

Thank you!

Sara Sutton

www.sarajsutton.com
authorsarasutton@gmail.com

ISBN: 978-0-578-43234-2
Library of Congress Control Number: 2018915159
Cover Photo by Bailie Maxwell
Cover Design by Sara Sutton
Printed in the USA

I dedicate

this book

to my soul family.

Those of blood and not,

far and near,

living and dead.

I am so thankful

to be here

with

you.

OF EARTH AND SMOKE

This book
is about
annihilation,
obliteration,
addiction
and
reincarnation.
The phoenix
rising from
the ashes
of dust and devastation.
Every soul
has its own journey
and this is mine.
I welcome you in
to the deepest love
of my life.

My soul
so loves
the hot breath
of human life.
The gentle dance of dawn,
or the comfort in the birds song
as the moon begins its rise.
Maybe my soul
has seen this all so many times;
perhaps it's even a little tired.
Yet each morning it feels
like all the stars
in the universe
are burning
just for me,
and I find myself
surprised

again to be,
here on earth.

I made this crown myself.
With feathers and shells,
flowers and stones.

I place this pinnacle
of pride upon my head
and know exactly
who I am.
Artemis; the Huntress,
the Goddess of the forest.

My soul craves
the call of the magpie,
the sound of river
and rustling leaves.
It is always the first
and the last

imprint in my mind.

I would come back
to Earth
1000 times
if I could devote
each second to our Mother
and the thirst
she creates in me.

As one reaches the top
of the mountain
only to ask,
what is beyond
the next ridge?

I went through
so many lives
looking for you,
endlessly until now.

I have been walking
and searching
the eyes of lovers -
is it you?

It was a thousand years and more-
lives lived short and long.
I passed through towns, created families,
but my soul always waited up at night
for you to come for me.

I searched and found love

but it wasn't yours.
I died and searched again,
endlessly,
til the end.

Kailey

Just last night,
I thought of things untouched.
Looked out the window
and felt the weight
of the heavy rain
as if it were on my own chest.
And it hasn't stopped,
not for a second.

2007

In my dreams
secrets are revealed to me;
untamed laughter
like smoke that drifts through the trees.
Untamed laughter,
like meandering mist on the sea's.
Gracefully falling,
like soft drops of rain
upon leaves.

Germany 2006

I assure you -

the Earth will hear of love.

And it will shake,

shifting of the tectonic plates.

Sister

I am a murderer, a martyr -

ruined by this life.

Forsaking all Gods,

I will worship her,

whose pain is

greater than religion.

The wolf sleeps

inside my chest.

Don't rest,

don't rest.

Something really strange
happens.
After a number of
days,
I begin to feel
(trapped, reckless,
ravenous)
with *only* the vision
of the forest
inside my mind.

As soon as I get there,
I stop to listen.
I hear the silence,
and finally
I can
breathe.

There is a beast in me.

Even if it takes

1000 lives, lived and died,

I'll come back

each time

with the same

voice inside my soul

telling me to find -

you.

Forgetting who I am -
I let your wave crash
extinguishing
that hot blood
that fire,
my soul.
Plato said that heat
equals life;
hot earth,
hot sun,
hot blood
and my river veins.
You've tried to kill
the killer in me
and all I have
are regrets
stacking up inside my body.

I wake up
from dreams of
peacock mating dances
against the dim light
of sunset.
I wake up
choking for breath.
We are made up
equally of light
and dark;
we choose which mark
to wear.
We are stardust, iron and water.
Lightning
is in our bones
and thunder
is our mind.

This

is

the most

sacred place

on earth:

where the ocean meets the shore.

Letting the earth speak,

we

step outside

at sunrise

to feel the light frost

covering everything.

That alone, is *enough*.

Your heart heavy, like a draping berry,

for years only God can count.

The ocean is here *for us*,

the most obvious and blatant reminder;

endure.

The morning call:

The birds

wake up

absolute

in their ecstacy -

shouting out their joy.

And now

their

bliss

exists

in me.

Where is the light
coming from?
Walk endlessly -
all your life
in that direction.

My body requires the sound

of the roaring, wide ocean.

The constant vibration

of crashing waves.

That call of the sea,

the infinite cry,

I imagine

is what the vast open

universe sounds like -

a comforting song

in the space between

our earth and heaven.

Dawn

We wake in the forest,
kissing the fern,
drinking the moss.
The golden light
shines
on the reaching pines.
This is the most
beautiful moment
in the universe:
the awakening of beings.

Something pulls you from inside,

like how the sail boat is pulled by the tide.

Like how the birds

know where to migrate,

and the fish - where to spawn.

The cycle itself is what we are seeking.

Certain seeds of trees won't grow

until they have been burned.

That is how we are.

Begging for the fire

to bring us to ash

and back to life.

When they ask nationality,

I say:

part God,

part human,

part stardust,

water

and ruins.

Everything opens

up to the light.

It acts as the

universal sign

for life

to wake,

sing,

bloom,

or grow.

Here's what I need to be happy:

the sound of birds.

I crouch down to listen,

looking out the window

I soak in the last sweet

yellows of sunset

to satisfy my heart.

I opened

up a space

inside my body

for the light

to come in

and because of that -

the butterflies in my stomach

still live.

Legs: for chasing the souls intent

Eyes: for seeing the invisible

The Heart: for bringing love into the Earth

Bones: for holding all the pain

Flesh: for dancing it away

The mind of humanity is opening -

like a pupil letting light in.

It was preordained,

destiny,

fate

for

us to remember,

at last.

Realizing DNA has memory

and energy has nothing to do

with what we have been taught.

If you don't believe in magic,

you haven't tried hard enough.

And the greatest secrets

of the universe

have been written

in notebooks like these.

Can I sit
and read you poetry
like I used to,
my souls friend?
My heart and yours
are one.
The remembrance
of lifetimes together
lingers like our
wild laughter.
We used to
run through the night
drunk with youth,
dancing.
Now my heart
hungers for those
nights;

unapologetically
lost in savage
happiness.

God knew
exactly
what I needed,
when she sent me
you.

Under the sun
souls pass
in and out
of this world.
Some say
it takes
millions of years
for the spirit
to spiral
back into unity
with God.
When you look
up high enough,
the galaxies spiral too -
along with the shell,
the snail,
the sunflower,

the storm.
How sweet
this all becomes
when you see life
in that light.

The vision of motherhood
keeps arriving.
I'm naming my children
before they are even
conceived.
I'm supposed
to be looking down
for the elk
but my eyes keep rising
towards the clouds.
I want to build a snowberry crown
for the both of us.
When I am a mother,
I will grow my hair long.
I will wear a high crown
in honor of my true self,
the creator of life.

The art of holding

the shattered pieces

together is delicate.

I suppose like the roots

standing up the

tree.

Gripping tight

against the

thrashing wind

and Earth's

unending gravity.

My spirit is a dancer,

ecstatically twirling,

in the universe of stars

moved, beyond control

by a spark-

the beginning of all days.

The dark bird of sunrise

attempts an approach,

perched on the shoulder of my life.

I've escaped her each time so far.

She risks everything

to try and ruin me.

But I know too much already

and she knows I would never

stop long enough

for her

to catch me.

Some days I'm entirely depleted.
I don't want to give.
I don't want to take.
I just want to be.
A perfect night, to me,
is a stunning sunset
and sitting silently
with a pen and paper.
How else can you see
what will come?
It's true -
you seek what seeks you.
You must take the step
to find

what's behind the breath,
what was always there,
careening ever so
slightly towards you
all this time.
That is how
love works
and poems
are written
and art
is made.

There are two women who live

inside of my mind:

one broken and bleeding

on her knees

and the other

standing over her

screaming

"GET UP"

We resemble the earth:
blue eyes - the ocean
tan skin - the sand
and blonde hair -
the color of beached driftwood.
Some have the forest in their eyes -
green as pine.
Some have skin the color of
red earth,
black earth,
brown earth.
Others have teeth like wolves,
hair like fire.
Our bodies move like fluid
the water that we come from.
Always returning
to the river

the lake
the sea.
We bloom like the flowers
and fall like the leaves.
All we can hope for
is to someday
become part
once again
of the warm,
sweet breeze.
And when ready -
let the soul
spill out of the body
like smoke
from a chimney.

I've been trying so hard

for so long

to forget.

Pleading desperately

with my mind

to forget -

to let

the visions fall away,

to let

the memories fade.

Forget the pain

that has made its way

up into my heart.

And alone,

at the end of each day

I patch the hole

that lets in the dark.

At once

I feel

the butterflies

release

in my stomach

and flutter up

into my chest.

I catch a quick gasp of air

as I prepare for the road ahead.

The wind is ushering me in

to where my soul can drink

and collect,

I live for the ascension -

upwards and over,

upwards and over.

This life: a steep ledge.

I anoint myself
before I sleep;
sweet orange oil,
lemongrass,
lavender.
A mixture of devotion-
to the great mystery,
to the racing wind.
I press my hands together
whispering
a few kind words
to my sunken heart.
I breath in
slow
and deep,
and release.

I am a divine being

realizing my own divinity.

Each day a new petal

of the flower

unfolds.

This is where the love begins,
right where the light comes in.
I look for you
in every face I see.
I look
down in the low valley,
up through the high peak.
You suck up the nectar of life
so that the sweetness
drips from your lips.
The flesh of the fruit
becomes my flesh -
two bodies forming one skin.

This art is my escape.

I try to leave those memories

drowning

in the tall grass of my mind

watching them fall behind

as I run towards

new life.

The beast that saves me:
I never had a father to teach me
to be strong like a redwood tree.
Strength I had to learn on my own.
Before he left, although,
he did put me in wrestling.
I fought so hard
I made all the girls cry,
then desperately apologized.
I didn't realize my own strength,
humans seldom do.
Until something so savage
happens
to create in you
the beast
necessary
to survive.

I let the whey
drain from the curds.

This is an honor,
not work.

We take the ingredients
of the earth,

to create
to birth

the recipe
for memories;

the mornings
in the barn

as the goats
labored on,

kissing the new life
that was already
so strong.

I've been trying to find
a way to say this:
(the thought is dangerous
and yet)
my mind won't let
the words
come out of my chest.

What if I keep climbing?
Letting earth and blood build
under my nails,
letting earth and blood build.

He raped your girlfriend
as he held a gun to your head,
you stuck a needle in your neck
all on the same bed.

I try to erase
your black
track marks.
I try to
wash you clean.

I will keep climbing,
letting earth and blood build
under my nails,
letting earth and blood build.

What was covered

is now exposed.

We stop to watch the tide

at the side of the road.

The earth breathes in water

and breathes out, an oath.

When mom was alive
and she would
sleep on your couch
every night,
I'd wake up
to feel her chest,
to make sure
there was still breath.
Make sure there
was still life left.
Hand on her heart
and my eyes closed
towards the sky,
please God don't take her
from me tonight.

Here is the problem for them:
I took the keys to my own power
and when
that happened,
there was no turning back.
I've learned how to dance
away my pain
and turn the abuse into strength.
It was the conditioning of my will
for a reason larger than myself
and the silence in my soul
only knows the reasons still.

The experiences
write themselves
inside you.
Creating an imprint,
a cosmic tattoo.
And you wear it
on the outside.
Letting the experiences
dictate your life.
But after a while
you decide
to learn
to work magic
and turn
the darkness
into light.

Mom

By days end, I'm exhausted
and turn my mind
to the many
things in life I love.
Snow covered mountains,
a hot fire, fresh caught fish.

We romanticise our most
celebrated moments -
when you love anything,
you immortalize it.

Is it the mind that recalls
or is it the heart?

Scents and sensations,
colors, crisp air and a breeze.

Either way,
your thoughts
too often
wander
back to the very same
moments -
playing them over
like a slide
again and again.
in your mind.

We wake
in the hours of dawn
to proceed into
the still silence
of the Earth,
to hunt
the land
for a scent
caught
years ago.
Following clues
left over
from the last life,
finding them
hiding among
the cliffs of your
heart.

How long
have all the answers
been waiting for you?
Tucked just beneath the surface,
a seed planted,
begging like a future child
for you
to allow it
to sprout.

The dark bird of sunrise
is becoming harder to escape.
I wake up devastated.
I turn my head
and see the bird perched,
determined.
I jump up and run.
Faster than I ever have before.
She's gaining on me;
I've gotten slower,
or her, faster.
She wants to destroy me.
She chases
and I run -
clinging to the light in my mind.
Begging myself
to never stop

to never slow -
bare feet
and dripping wet
lungs dropping,
gasping for breath.

True North

Inside,
has always been
an essence of stillness
that I come back to;
my True North.

Life has a lot of crossed out lines
and half hatched eggs.
I wonder -
how did I get blessed
with this stillness?
Such a direct route
back to center.

The stillness
is my first destination
and my last.
It is my
waking,
my sleep
and everything
in between.

The soul seeks -
as is the nature of the spirit.
We are little pieces of God
trying to find itself.
We are sand made from rock;
particles circling a center.

We are best friends
but have forgotten -
now asking,
"what's your name?"
And when they speak their name
all of the sudden you see it.

This was a mile marker,
a lantern post you set
for yourself,

a thread tying it all together.

Guided by
the hand of the wind
we are here
to find *our* way.
To unite our mind
with our heart
giving flame to the spark
leaving beauty in our path,
eradicating darkness
as we dance.

I myself

have lived

a million lives before.

And I'll live a

million lives more,

before the sun burns out.

On one side
of the earth
the orange sun
is setting in the west.
On the other -
the periwinkle blue
and pink full moon
is rising in the east.
The moon has spent
millions of years
chasing the sun;
precise, devoted, undaunted.
We all hope to realize
a love like that.
To find a force that arrives
always and forever
by our side.

The moon so adored
the sun that the
universe gave them
to us as our example of
pure love.

We see how frail they are

and know we will be frail

like them

(far sooner

than we think).

It's true, what they said,

it all happens in just a blink.

So we say firmly to ourselves

and to the world:

we will swim

when it comes time

for us to sink.

This life has emptied me out.

I want to write your name

on the trees

hollowing them -

leaving them cleft like me,

a message sending you home

through the trail of

my falling leaves.

I'll never
get enough
of the blue spruce
at sunrise.
The pink lingers
on top
of the ocean's horizon
like a thick sea fog;
a wandering mist.
With each moment
the sunrise transforms
and shifts,
beckoning
the pastel purples
and final blues
as the
full light of day moves closer.

The sunrise
is like dessert,
except it comes first.
It is the climax in every lover,
the peak of every mountain.
It is the most
honored gift
of Earth.

I tell myself,
she is no longer here.
And someday
I
will no longer be here.
I tell myself to prepare,
to welcome
the sunset of souls
and
submit, as the plants do
when the time arrives,
to the cold wind of night.
We must not be sad
when the time comes
to run off the cliff
of life
into the ocean

of death.
We must remember
the crickets and clover
and the wings of the white crane
- all the happiest
moments we have ever made.

My life consists

of rivers and streams

honey and bee's,

a forest full of bleeding hearts,

wild flowers

and eagles.

We must renounce

all Gods but the Earth.

Tonight,
at dusk,
glancing out
at the distant hills,
my nose caught the scent
of winter field grass
mixed with the sweet molding of leaves.
It is a rare occasion
for the wind to mix just right.
It was one of those
perfect moments in time.
We stack the years up in our lives
searching this earth for happiness
and in the end,
only to realize
it's found in moments like this.

The sweet ache of being human:

We are a soul that dies
and begs God
like a stubborn child
to let it come back,
just once more,
for the
hundredth time,
regardless
of the pain
and ripping sadness of earth.

We've only got so long

to crack the code

of life

and time

wrinkles everything,

especially the mind.

I am the goat farmer
in the misty hills of Sardinia,
aging cheese
and my soul's intent
in the fire smoke.
I am the gypsy in India
charming snakes,
dancing in the night
with skin hot to the touch
and dusty feet.
I am the soldier in battle.
Running to keep alive,
and leaving the dead behind.
I am the deck hand,
the captain,
the sea
and the ship.

I am the shepherd,
the pasture and the lamb
within it.

The spirit

has always been

my subject of study,

fiercely driven

by a homesickness.

Discovering parts of myself

like land I've known

but long forgotten.

My entire life
I've wanted
to crawl into a ball of light.
I surrender, life won.
I feel the pain you carry
and I want it to quit.
I want to shed it like a skin -
and turn my attention
to something more comforting,
something more alive.
The pain has run its blade
so deep through my life -
I've become desperate
to escape it, to evade it.
At times I can outrun it,
but only for a moment.
Then quickly

she's on me
again:
the dark bird of sunrise.
It's said everything happens for a reason,
and I'm just dying to know
what all this means -
this life,
my praying hands,
their needles thin.

You were the best dream
I'd had in a long time.
Maybe the best
dream of my life.
But always a dream,
somewhere out of reach
and it was all my own fault -
because
I could have you if I want.
And I do,
I crave you
from somewhere
so deep
in my stomach

that I am no longer
hungry for food.
Starving
as I sit
with him
writing poems
about you.

The strawberries
will spread
forever
if you let them.
Falling down
from the berry box
to the ground.
Collecting sweetness,
(aren't we always)
as one
then two
berries,
turns into
a mound.

I was never
meant
to be
anything
similar
to ordinary.
I am meant
to make
of my life -
a work of art.

When you
look in my eyes
you will see,
it is not
just me -
I hold
the Universe
in my being.

It feels like
my body is filled
with toxic waste -
and then
the music plays.

I can dance
on top of every
horrible experience
I've ever had -
stomping them down
into the thirsty ground.

With every twist

of my hips,
each flick of my wrist,
I throw off
the heart ache.
And like magic
the ache is gone.

And I dance -
with the butterfly strength
of all the women
that have passed
through this earth.

Your life
is like
a sequence
of fireworks
and I always
end up getting
burned.

The only
thing I want
to scream
my name
is the spine
of a book.

The light falls
upon all:
woman or man.
Open your eyes
and the palm
of your hand.

I want to go
to a place
where all I can see
is the tips of trees.
Elated
and
elevated.

I have been
writing poems,
forming shields
out of them -
building up my
protection.

As a partner
you disappointed me
so continuously.
I'd make up all the reasons
for you
when I knew,
there was no excuse.

It felt like
it was killing me
but actually
it was making me
more alive:
waiting for this moment
to arrive.

Warrior women:
God knows
I am
what the world needs,
that is why
she is here
with me.

When you
are accustomed
to life being
so hard,
it feels like thievery
for anything
to come
easily.

The love I have
for life
is the same
as the love I have
towards a lover.

My heart plods on,
trying to control
the excitement,
the wonder.

Like food, we crave
our family,
our friends

and the memories
we forge together
like steel in fire.

And finally -
come the days on the coast.
Growing up next
to the sea
all my life,
makes any coast line
feel like home.

We celebrate the crab,
the oysters,

the delicate tastes
of the ocean.
We savor them,
like we savor
our seconds,
like we savor
the presence
of the wind and
her salty breath.

I'm writing poems
in my sleep now,
waking up mid dream
to write them down.

The image is foggy
but I am trying to catch it -
before the words are lost
to another world,
to a space in my mind
I can only reach
sometimes.
Collecting the words
in the deepest state of rest

knowing
this is how
the universe
converses with
and urges
my soul.

There are certain things
there is no point
in talking about.
I'm clearly broken,
but you want me to
elaborate
on the separated
pieces
individually.
You want me to open up
and show you
what I've been trying to bury.

I don't.

I don't want to talk about
her.
I don't want to tell you,
to admit,
that some things
never get better,
they just never do.
But still
you
have to live -
but still
you
must
live.

In the pitch dark forest

I sleep,

with the wolf skin

wrapped around me.

I love the
red branches
of the bare
blueberry plants
in winter.
They must enjoy
this resting state.
It can't be easy
to give such sweetness
so selflessly
in the long summer heat.
We all at times
exist in two ways:
bare and blossoming.
There *is* beauty in both.

My heart -

resting on the wings

of a hawk

all my days.

We are a new kind of being.

We bend when we are

supposed to break,

we live when we are left to die.

There is no question,

no doubt

from my toes

to my eyes -

we were put here

to push through

and let love rise.

Hidden behind the trees

is the bay.

With no one to notice

or give credit

to how much life thrives

in that grey marshy inlet.

All the creatures exist

quietly, fond of being forgotten about -

relying on their ability

to live

without

being noticed.

The world marched on too quickly,

thankfully.

Leaving the bay behind the trees

somewhere lost in time.

That is how

the wild places survive.

I'll be there

at the end of time

when all this is through -

standing, smiling

waiting for you.

I'm not sure

how much more

I can lose

and still live.

When you see

the gull fly

you'll know

you are

home.

Seducing your pain:

It's a chemical reaction,

like something that once tasted

bitter but now is sweet.

Somewhat like water

changing forms

in different environments.

Similarly you

feel the pain and transform the energy

using these sacred techniques.

Not everyone understands

what this means.

Thankfully, not everyone

has had to bare so much pain

that the only choice left

was to learn to love it

and defeat it.

It thought it would destroy me

but I came out laughing.

Because I so easily

seduced the pain

and reduced it to nothing.

One me died

as another was born.

And it wasn't sad or bitter

or cold,

it was strong,

glowing and warm.

I fantasize

about waking up

alone.

With no one to lecture,

or complain.

No one to control me,

tell me I'm lazy

for sleeping so late -

it's only 8.

Or that I'm bitchy

because I'm sleepy

as you stand above me

talking

always talking.

I want to wake alone

in silence.

Put my two feet on the ground

as I get out of bed

with no one but myself to please.

I do not want to be sick with worry

about how I can ease

your mind.

Easing my own mind is work enough,

but I've been last on my list for years.

I'm done with that.

I'm first.

I sleep when I want,

wake when I please.

My only concern is me.

My soul

was forged

deep

in the smoldering

fire coals.

Sealing in

a molten mixture

of earth

and smoke.

Thank You

49749174R00074

Made in the USA
Columbia, SC
27 January 2019